Rockclimbing in Silk

To the memory of my parents
John Rhydderch (1936-1994)
Angharad Rhydderch (1939-1996)
who taught me to read Homer

SAMANTHA WYNNE RHYDDERCH

Rockclimbing in Silk

seren

seren
is the book imprint of
Poetry Wales Press Ltd
Nolton Street, Bridgend, Wales
www.seren-books.com

© Samantha Wynne Rhydderch, 2001

The right of Samantha Wynne Rhydderch
to be identified as the Author of this Work
has been asserted in accordance with the
Copyright, Designs and Patents Act, 1988.

ISBN 1-85411-298-8

A CIP record for this title is available from
the British Library

*The publisher works with the financial assistance of the
Arts Council of Wales*

Cover Image: detail of a photograph by Helen Sweeting

Printed in Palatino by
Bell & Bain Ltd, Glasgow

Contents

Rockclimbing in Silk

wasn't something she'd intended
from the start.
The castle's finger
beckoned jaggedly.
I blame the sky
or the unconsoled sea,
the wind bandaging
the towers.

The seagulls, disenchanted
with the penitentiary,
mimed agony,
fought off the sun
that forced her down
among the irises,
the uncertain air
in her throat.

Closer

Five hundred yards the sea said the estate agent
ten years ago. Now the edges of the garden
have frayed into the waves. Every night
the tide gnaws at the briars in the drive.
Coastal erosion, the cancer of the west.

From outside you'd never guess
at the severed floor under the dining room carpet
unless you stepped into the bay window
for a better view. Year after year
the photograph alters: more water, fewer trees.
Part of its charm smiles the agent.

The windows dribble dark cracks
that intimidate the onslaught of moss.
Shale inches down the path
to the lure of the rock. Insignificant glint,
divider of salt, preserve the falling.

A slate tilted on the gutter, that's all
it will take. Buy this house, wake up
in silt, a mouthful of clay,
with your bedroom shipwrecking above.
Twenty yards the land. Nothing like slippage
to take your breath away.

The Lighthouse Keeper's Daughter

was the first to see the dead musician's
eyes at dawn, blue and immense

as Llangorse Lake where his voice
would echo from water to rock to

water. That was before the migraines
bleached her tongue, combing her skull

each night until mute with pain she
polished cobalt vowels in the wind.

The whiteness throbbed round
and round, firm and eternal as

this glass tower, a prism
practising madness: light, limb, dark,

blade, light, clover, dark, lake, light,
dark, wound, dark, dark.

Paramilitary Lover

He strokes my neck like the barrel of a rifle
he might have killed that German with,
his boots by the door, susceptible to the cold.
I glow by the fire in tandem with
the rosewood dresser, impartial to flames,
me with a passion for granite, him
with his head shaved against the night,
shedding his armour plate by plate.
I sleep under his shield, enfolded
in an English flag I think will
become my shroud. While I thrill
among the lilies, placing a chestnut
on the grate like a move in chess,
I see the incentive of lace
defeat artillery hands down.

One Way Ticket

The glass he drinks from
darkens at his lips
as the ship shudders

out. Another sip,
his anodyne is working.
Instinct makes me wonder

whether it will be fast
or slow. I see him dissect
his troubles at the railing

as he peels the flaking paint.
Reams of thought in copper plate
stream in the seagulls' wake.

His monocle trembles as he
still sees the blue between
the pines at Soar-y-Mynydd,

still hears the shot,
still hears the shot.

First Aid Class

I kneel there with the head gardener in my arms,
feeling the pulse in his neck the way he touches
leaves in real life, his skin a series of impressions
on calico beside me. Everyone an iridologist
dressing head wounds with the enthusiasm
of the starched in field hospitals before 1915.

We learn that fainting is merely the rearrangement
of blood, my bronchial tree simply a cameo of me,
but more vitriolic. I am eager to see the cyanosed
around the edges, intuit a cardiac arrest.
Now and then I hear the thrum of a defibrillator,
arterial gestures from the past. Handling a rib-cage
over lunch I have a sense of ornament.
Finally we study a handout of unconsciousness,
poison ivy groping at the window panes.

I imagine us meeting under other circumstances,
coy about our intimacy. Then I begin to understand
the way surgeons avoid the resuscitated
in *The Lamb & Flag*, the gardener playing cribbage
something too abstract, why terminology matters:
"terracotta" to "red", "episode" only a dot
on a screen.

We are asked to elevate a limb: the rituals of a sacrament,
the illustrations in the manual mute in savagery
as my hands around those open veins.

The X-Ray Room

I am dismantled in monochrome
on the screen opposite the student doctors,
their gaze moving from me here to

me translated into porcelain
there. I am Exhibit A, my symmetry
unmasked by this cut and paste version

of my guts hermeneutically sealed
in negative. I stand by my parallel
text as if to elucidate

evisceration. My bones
in triplicate have nowhere to hide.
Their fragility becomes heraldic

when these exegetes invoke them
in Latin. You see, my other
has been deceiving me all along.

The Electric Chair

dreams of holding you
bright, your metal tongue
singing white notes
to us safe behind glass,
watching you fizz

in its embrace, your past
intact as ice.
I know the bar we pose at
like nervous dancers
won't ignite as you

thrill and burn, terrifying
anemone in its arms.

On Leave

This is a dream: here is a barn
white against the night
under a Magritte moon,
a crucifixion looming
from its rafters, a draught
intoning a new tune, a shaft
of light inside the palm.

You are thinking in mazurkas
across the courtyard, across the cobbles
stained with wine. Mine
is that banquet, that jigsaw
in the windows, pink wings
flitting at every glass,
the cast speaking in Gauloise.

Now it's all an aeon away:
this is gin and tonic land
at thirty-five thousand feet.
I'm putting my watch back
seventy-two hours, and waiting
for another walk-on part,
a century from now.

Pope Gregory XI's Bedroom

He has rhyming wallpaper
with parakeets on green tendrils.
Over his bed stretch

ostrich feathers arching
into a dome he dreams he'll see again
one day, down south.

From his stone windowsill he'll
fit a convent in his ring
where six pray daily in their cells

that he won't choke on quails
or lose his throne to some Italian
jerk. He muses on how best to

silence her, that odd Dominican who
writes continually, insisting that he
give it up, come back to Rome.

At night he crushes eggshells between his teeth,
sees the Rhône swirling below,
deep, filled with his own blood, slow.

Julia

She's down there in the cellar,
my rival, propped up against the wall,
a series of eerie lines on canvas.
He's almost painting her lips — burnt mauve,
the colour of the sand from my window
under a threatening sky.

Every day her eyes seize me
more intently than before — they know
something I can't, details sealed in oil
as he soothes them at dusk.
Her smile flickers up through the floorboards
as if she will say that word I can't
bear to hear: his name.

Instead I say it first,
paint my lips, kiss
the mirror, then
devour him.

Flavia's Curtains

Verecundus rarely screwed the housemaid
twice in one day more like six times
an hour if he could she thought
but no one really knew and anyway
who cares if he can't keep
his toga on what with the price of corn
and purple curtains hard to come by
nowadays and the latest war up north
and that poor poet Ovidius banned
to the Black Sea for being in love.
Won't green do?

Miss Rivet

I bore strangers into corners of bars
with tales of my four lost loves.
They sit polite to the point of madness
as I unfold my familiar litany: David's
eating habits, Paul's terrible dress sense,
Ged's traumatic childhood with his auntie
in Birkenhead. I leave nothing to the imagination.
Bryan? Yes, he was one of them too.
Not that I'd have known. Trouble is
they all blend into one another. The thing
they had in common was they all liked a good chat.
What? Oh no, you see, what I have to say is
so unusual. I take up hours of people's time.
Of course they want to know. Then there's my
medical history: catatonic states and autistic
tendencies. I usually fill them in on that too.
All connected really. Next stop *The Royal Oak*.
I know the landlord's heard it all before,
but the language students devour every word.

Lighting the Fire

Temperamental, I know you will do nothing until
your bed is made up. I give you one match, like a word
and you will talk all evening. You take possession
of my jewels as you draw yourself up. You want them all
for yourself and I let you, with my raw dependence on heat.
You eat and eat as if you have some rare disease.
You're an addiction in yourself — I could stay by your side
all night. If I placed no limits on you, I know you'd
take over the whole house. You're so demanding
you and your dust, yet I fall for you every time,
the unregimented smell of chopped pine
in the grate.

Self Portrait in Ice

Side A

The polished floor tells me I can.
First of all the mountains terrify in white
through the casement. Then the lake
with its thick membrane lying
strict at the edge of the garden.
I'll need a compass to start.
Wreathed in frost I chart my way
to where there was water,
sepulchral breath columbine
at the shore.

Ornamental in my semi-state livery,
a blade on each foot, I think I was decorated
in peacetime. One skate on the lake.
At home, the cutlass chair drawn up
to the fire, room service, antimacassars,
a wallpaper called *Before Dark.*

I scar the lake's immaculate face, the miracle
of standing on liquid. From here,
the rockery is fractional alabaster, my legs
seamless aluminium, unconscionable mermaid.
I am writing a love sequence as I
wheel and ring the whole valley.
This is what it means, the madness
and tranquillity of ice. My monograph
must begin.

Side B

Stagefright with geraniums. Perpendicular,
I sense autobiography
on ice. Some kind of chrome revival
perhaps: cavalry, a sky the colour of
gunmetal, my lake, my palimpsest.

No side effects, just me updating my wounds
in unscheduled snow. I write my name
with my feet, assailed calligraphy, inverted
nineteenths with full military honours. Three sheets
to the wind, I am water-haunted
on a surface as intransigent
as history. In Wordsworth's day
women couldn't skate. Instead men
pushed them around the frozen lake
on chairs; that's what it says
in the exhibition. For *couldn't*, read
wouldn't, shouldn't, mustn't.
Modality wasn't their strong point
in the eighteenth century.
Now we just have autotext: does it all
for you. Hypocryphal really.

Fading, the light. Where the sun picks them out
the garden paths are alluring as cinema aisles.
Goodbye, zero-rated lake, cataplectic, you hold
trade secrets, not to be taken
on consecutive nights. All the King's horses
have come to take me away, minus
the diamond, the mast in two at my feet.
Esyllt and her crossbow-seagull nailed
to the helm, I sail my way through
the archipelago, the treachery of ice.

Rituals At Our Peril

It's Tuesday. He's Robert Burns again
tonight — he got the mid-week
slot. The tourists pursue him
down alleyways and courtyards
where he serenades people in their flats
with a running commentary
on the six o'clock news, a sort
of meta-narrative they time their stir-fry by.
The residents of Lady Greystairs' Close
know all about when Burns left his wife and
why and what Edinburgh meant
to him. It means nothing to them, all this
poetry and playacting for the Japanese
to video and show to Aunty Nang
next week in Yokohama. This man
who is bathed in another man's drama
has become their sunset, their part-time
Romeo charming high windows
in eight floor tenements. So yes,
we lose ourselves to rituals
at our peril.

The Phonebook Errata

This is a recorded message
from BT: we'd like to apologise for
omitting all the bachelors this year.

So these are the ones who got away —
the undialled, the deleted, the disconnected,
the illegible, the eligible who ticked the wrong box,
foxed BT with an odd surname
or an unpronounceable address.
They didn't expect to be
ex-directory. It was a free gift after
they became temporarily unavailable.
All those digits losing their
touch in drawers remain
unbilled, lineless, unobtainable,
constantly hung up. Perhaps they'll
get a better reception next year.

If you find yourself in any way
affected by this error, we advise you
to press your star button twice
now.

Deacon Brodie's Predecessors

I. Controversial ticket arrangements

He is leading me into the Brae Chantry in chainmail.
The Pentatonic scale predicts that he will
keep his word. I am drunk on elderflower wine
and the parapets trap my plaits, Guinevere
on shiny paper in my standard issue headdress.
This is carbon dating. I am in a state of advanced frailty,
impressed by his pecs. All strappy with my
head injuries, the crewelwork holds my gaze until he
lifts his visor. Carreg Ateb, Red Rackham's treasure,
said the stones, she's a replica Portia, a windlass,
once opaque on Snake Pass, formerly babe of
Llanbedrog. He, local butcher turned knight,
the rural pile, a house called *Isabel:* that's where
I live I do, on the Holy Mile, royal to the point of
compassionate pageantry.

II. The Surf Report

David Penhaligon in the Blackwaterfoot Hotel.
He was a fair size stag, Invercauldie craver,
dragons slain at no extra cost:
an elaborate date. I was King Arthur's love-rat
in a rattan chair: simply add boiling water.
Look at the text again, Phoebe. There's no surcharge
on November Island, Ynys Tachwedd.

Then there was Angus McGillivray, well baronial,
indulging with me in horizontal collaboration,
the flagpole fittings shining. I think he thought I was
one of those computershell blondes he'd met years ago
in the *Old Sea Lock*, stripping wood with affection.
He's someone I'm not too patio about — should have been
marinated in apostrophes. A vulture's got more
bedside manners. So, furnish me with the relevant
afternoon and I'll complete the dot to dot.

Been under a preservation order for a while now,
me and Dave Penhaligon, the Court Stenographer.
Pillar talk with lemons. He was the one who painted the
mural in Talybont. It was a get-out clause really.

Before the war we drank in *Tafarn Jem*, enjoying a bit of
quality isolation, Wensleydale and Bourbon,
a right caryatid I was. They live for the *Jif*
all those cariads behind the bar.
The good thing about the plastic ones is that
they stay yellow forever.

III. Swordfish glamour

The dusk is flexible, so I can go now if I want.
I can suppurate on an ottoman in the *Packet* with
Dr Finckelstein finishing her latest book
while I try to locate my *De Priester*
offshore fasteners. In the event of sickness, please call
the cabin crew for assistance. Always resisted that one —
said a Hail Mary instead in Heol Mary Ann.
I think he noticed my arabesque inlay. I've been fairly
sympathetically renovated. There's a girl in the mirror wants
a word, Dave. I wore a sail cut on the bias that night.
Got a purchase on that? I think he was impressed by my
learning: I've read all fourteen volumes of the
West Wales Hysterical Records. Volume Ten is the best:
the origins of laverbread and two-tone troubadours.
Trivial yet riveting. Trimmed all me wicks
the same night. Now I've got a lightbulb called *Sylvania*.
When the wires writhe I do my rebound therapy
in a helicopter. It's a shortcut to the north wind.
                                        I translated it all
into Coralese for him. Then I documented him
losing consciousness. He had quite an aerial view of me.
The Shepherdess Position. It was in the Dan Stâr,
a cupboard to die in that, flush with the wall and a
chipped sycamore mirror and all.

IV. Fragment (no suggestions)

There's a stringless harp
in the garden. My sister used to be a siren
too. Now she lives in a semi-detached
castle with a ligature and plays garage anthems
on Saturday nights, herringbone bedspreads
in the spare rooms.

V. Madder

Suffering from word stress, a cumulative effect.
Used to do chromolithography on Mynydd Sylen,
me herbs coming on nicely, voice prompts in formaldehyde.
Dial listeria to hear my chalet: panel beaters on hexagonal
                                                    tables,
millinery issues, synthetic outrage etc. — a linen event.
It's hard to tell my life from your silhouette. I had a trellis
education, you see, all cacti and aquatics. Then I met a
high voltage pianist who was good at acquiring prepositions.
He was on the Storm Warning Committee.
I had a violin relationship with him, but he was fraught with
lavender. I spotted his emerging diagnoses
yonks before the medical profession even
bleedin' invented them. Diminishing returns.

VI. The Electoral Scrutineer

I was a woodcut in those days and he was my kind of thorn,
Paths and I. Foxtrot with digestives, aviaries, car tax,
cave paintings: we talked it all out. I was quite chicane
with my coriander hairdo, but I could tell from his
throat flora he was only in it for the
porcelain. I spelt out the rubrics, tried to create the right
ambulance, but he'd already read my
dental records. He wasn't up to the ink
and bleach technique either: chaotic disinfectant.
Time for your catafalque, laddie, forward, slash!

VII. Deacon Brodie

Say it with airfields,
with moon-embossed noise.

Think lampshade, opaline
as an attic salver.

I read it in the tide timetable,
his coming, a satin investiture

floodlit in the chandlery.
I was listing heavily,

wired for sound with regular clippings
and bunting, tuned in to his dragoon

elphinstone. The ruched blue
velvet drapes in the mess dealt me

a strong hand the night those
evening hills rolled ochre.

He'd been out at his forensic petroleum
again when he drew me in

to a doorway, all cloak and dagger while I
was incomplete seaweed

looking for value-added gravadlax
on a lattice keyboard.

He is the amethyst I sensed in the heather,
his military hardware enough to

infiltrate my split skirt narratives
infinitively.

Report

Of how I slept with an open map by the bed
all night, tracing his past like a detective
in my dreams, inhaling placenames he'd mentioned
over a drink that evening, hoping they'd thrive
merely though sleep, seep into veins, these words.
Ancestry like geography is a blur, white
as a main road, blue as a moonlit cove.

Writing becomes a requirement, a dial
on the gauge of inevitability.
Each morning the ache unfurls, a refusal
to be rolled up in a winding-sheet, wholly
alive, elaborate as needlework, full
blooded as a matador intricately
trussed under the hot afternoon sun, ready.

Farmyard Mirrors

They will take you by surprise on backroads,
bereft of dressing tables, lurching from hedges,
rejected, astute, crucial at bends, luring
tractors out of lanes, blotched with mildew.

The glamour they once absorbed whole, glints
tarnished. How they long to hold the glow inside
a bedroom window, feel the heaviness of drawers,
be polished, strung with necklaces,

not nettles. Indisputable, ever-admiring at dusk,
frowning at dawn, their loyalty always presumed
upon. Such fall from grace would be unthinkable
to those who carved their fluted legs,

to the organdie runners pressed
under a thick rectangle of glass, stains of
L'Air du Temps official as the bindweed is now.
How could the spectrum of reflection

invite such a betrayal? Weather permitting
the farmyard mirrors will survive two more
decades of deterioration, deflection on location,
before a recognition scene disappears forever.

Window Dressing

The frame large as my picture window at home
with its acre of sea, here in Amsterdam
we look in at her combing pale hair, curtained

by a drape plush as blood, a huge bed untouched
and pure as a museum piece, six dildoes
lined up on the mantelshelf like school prizes.

In the shop next door artificial fingers
point to a sky clear as the canal waters
that hold seven-storey houses upside down.

I enter a tulip stall, in awe and bound
by the glamour of petals. When I come out
I am holding a bunch of wooden flowers.

They will never die, unlike he whose tombstone
I lay them on now, his fibreglass leg gone cold.

Pin-up in the Cemetery

One glance at breakfast
then she's left to rot,
her tombstone a dustbin lid
until airborne she
launches herself at yew trees
and lych-gates. Tomorrow
another pair will resist
reading. Behind the railing
other bodies expose themselves
under grey slabs. Their final
statistics advertised in stone
titillate only the wind.
Something else erodes
their dignity, widens cleavages
year by minute.

The Embalmer

Slowly she smooths his face, his arms,
his torso on his velvet bed,
breathes into his ear, her fingers
combing his hair, delineates
his eyebrows through his stare.

She kneads his thighs, supervised
by the lilies above his head,
then deftly moulds his lips into a rose,
brushing his eyelids closed,
coaxing him into an immaculate sleep.

He insulted her once in the street,
this decapitated cretin who
gives himself up to the touch
of a stranger. She disarms him, parts
his hair for the first time and the last,
unsheathes her knife.

A Visit to the Footbinder

Beauty is in the toes they said
on my fifth birthday when I smiled
amidst the lotuses and said yes, yes
please, please make my feet smaller,
and even smaller yes than my almond eyes
stepping out towards their adolescent dance.

Still today I fear the smell of tobacco,
feeling it curl round my feet
in his dark cellar with the yellow light
peeling from the walls, staining his fingers
as he deftly breaks the bridges, folds back
the toes and binds them up.

In half-bitten nightmares, I am stumbling
through brittle fields of lotuses
with my hands tied behind me.

Part of the Furniture

Since I had him stuffed
and mounted in a glass case,
my husband has truly become
what he always was:
part of the furniture.
Addicted to sitting still and staring
out of the window, now I've made sure
he can do that permanently.
I know he'd thank me for it.
Always wanted to be on display,
in his best waistcoat, the centre
of attention. Suits him: far better
disembowelled than drivelling on.

The Embroiderers' Outing

You're allowed to have reservations
said the cameraman on the Clyde,
passing canapés as we curved towards

a barge in time to see the embroiderers
fierce at work. He zooms in while I
focus my telescope. Then a girl turns

and pricks her thumb when a vase
of crimson tulips falls and blurs,
her face tinted with disbelief behind glass,

preserved. I'd thought it was all gone:
devotion, the dutiful birds
woven and signed by this my hand

Susannah McPherson, the ninth day of
March, eighteen eighty-five. He shoots.
Prayers and geometric ivy still
turn yellow in parlours, draw no blood.

The Art Restorer

Years of walking past these episodes
in weekly boyhood rituals

had taught him nothing, but now
he lives with miracles and haloed acts,

full-scale trilogies in slow-motion;
the eyes, the mouths, the unspoken

conversations stoppered by paint.
It is not their bright robes

that seduce his eyes' detailed care,
but the days of dusty,

unsaid thoughts, the unsought
intimacy of a world condensed

to a dome, where his arms fathom
gravity. Reanimating

outstretched hands, a match is struck
in his grey heart like a miner

chipping away at the dark.
He is forced to pray when he

encounters these compressed
lives. Motionless, he

retouches his own life, emerges
from centuries under a veneer.

The Ballroom

I wash her bridal body, weak and white
in a shroud of institution sheets.

Naked in pearl earrings at ninety
she lies paralysed, her glass eye

fixed on a photograph where she
laughs in Vienna,

caught unambiguously
in a sepia waltz with some man

who stands frozen in mid-cigar.
I retrace her features

as she did the night she poured
herself into a mirror for him. Now

he sleeps in stone, waiting
for his stiff Eurydice to turn

again in a swathe of silk, vermilion lips,
hold her breath, vanish

beneath that cut-glass
chandelier.

Perfect Tense

Your jawline breaks the sky's azure field
like an axe. Jagged Ukrainian consonants
shatter onto your plate. I realign them

one by one in my head until they
form a new pattern, collapse
into a series of blue triangles. I hear

your syntax like a song in an archway.
Why shouldn't the sound of silver
defer that translation we'll never achieve?

As you turn your face to the hills,
the distilled intricacy of stonework
unfolds into a conversation beneath

your feet. My chaperone expounds
vigorously waving towards the cliffs. His Gaelic's
not quite up to it, I'd say. He's re-mythologised you

completely, an unwanted ventriloquist.
You insist on your own glossary. I hear
a past imperfect now where before

there were only relentless inflections
disappearing over the crags. I could not
retrieve them without an irreversible crash

into the sea. My decoder comes to a halt.
Another voice oozes out of the walls
like moss, velvet and whole. It is my own
drowning the lines set in stone.

Père Lachaise

A tilting virgin offers me a snowball
as I pass, but I
could never accept such transience in the palm.
Her eyes are sealed with lichen,
her smile bites a century's feigned
indifference, and those cracked wings
ground her between inscriptions.

It's far, this sound of stone
that mitigates the frost.
A bare shroud holds us numb
and voiceless as Edith Piaf
locked up inside her porchway.
Reliquaries crowd us out.
Their letters bleed green.

The Café Excelsior, Montmartre

Their fingertips touch
under an Art Deco lamp
pouring honey onto his blurred lips.
She can't speak any more —
the Chablis has gone to her head.
Instead she peels the silk scarf
from his neck and strangles
it between anaemic fingers.
Her mahogany eyes are haloed
by chandeliers
which dazzle him. He can't stop
searching, scrutinizing
the negative of himself
in the Steinway, its lid an open coffin
breathing out magnetic notes
like Sirens that have plunged him
into his own whirlpool.
But you, you are embedded in me
like a rusty nail.

Indiscretions

Opposite the *Parc St Jacques*
each cube of light
invites the evening in.
Henri in his shirtsleeves
soothes a wrought-iron balustrade.
On the second floor Mme Fougères
feeds her poodle with revolting
devotion, ignoring the husband who
wilts behind *Le Figaro*.
Below, Jean-Yves admires his twin
spattered with shaving foam,
turns out the light and crashes
into the *ascenseur*. Next door,
Mlle de Reuilly's shadow pulls out
her pins one by one. Hair falls
to her elbows as Jean-Yves enters
the *métro*. On the *troisième* Bernard's
come home with someone new.
The way he strips the cuticle
from his garlic tells you his
gratin dauphinois isn't the only thing
that tastes good.

Her Voice

For six months after you rang, I trapped your voice
in the answering machine, pouting the same new year
                                                greetings
in June. The modulations I know as shot silk
ceased. Your phrases became predictable
as a favourite song, a welcome set of phonemes
at the end of the day.

It was only later when I wanted to respond,
I realised how still they were,
your whispered sibilants, a trivial semiotic,
how near, how far.

Regency

His tricorn tilted, black-masked in a silk frockcoat,
the Hawkman bears down on me across the hall:
                                    I flick open my fan
and remember what the glossators intimated

about being mentioned in dispatches: east is east.
It was in the mezzotint footage I noticed him first:
quicksilver love, this master litigator and his one-dimensional

Aylesbury Sierra seven years ago, eleven lords a-leaping
while I was waiting on the tarmac, braid in the interim,
the centrefold of Hellebore Blood Boulevard.

He glided across Atlantic Ballroom, a statue
of Hecuba convulsing on the wall, Ski Queen Fondue,
www.bitterwaitress.com.

That was Congregation Day in the Zinc House yard,
day of career motet and index-linked muscavado.
Mine was the Shrievalty of Devon, an asphodel.

Ever since the watermelon it's been low-key largo
and pond accessories. If you are tequila-minded
you could see me expose my ephemera

on candlelit Battlefield Tuesday, drooping with mascara
and cartographers under a multiple-choice pergola.
I had him verbatim in the candle-making workshop

some disenchanted evening gazing at the aquarelles
with typical gunroom etiquette. Anecdotal
if you ask me. Margarine lies.

Take your tragedy and divide by three: the incisions
in his fingers deliberate as alcoves in mint. All I wanted was
a rank and file viola. Good thing I took the scenic

route. Close encounter or near miss? Couldn't tell you.
I was knocking back the pink water when he gave me
a piece of state coral in the village of Downstairs Binding.

Railway sleepers. I love it.

Blackshaw Head in the Wind

They discuss land at the bar. I drain my glass.
Remnants of binliners screech in the trees
like crows. The houses are brutal by twilight,
the colour of the moon intravenous as your voice
on the mobile, adjectives flickering on the moors
like house lights in the valley below.

The greenery a brocade at the cemetery gate,
I am scoured down to bare quartz,
forced across the church wall. Wind traps my breath.
The gravestones rise like accusations I can't
answer. I've seen them leering at me
in nightmares — that begonia feeling.
I mean strictly ballroom, but galeforce.

Willow Pattern

When you dropped the plate, the bridge broke
in two and the tiny blue ferns were torn.
Like us they would not mend. They spoke
in their dismembering; we could not mourn.
I wrote your name in willowy
handwriting on a scrap of paper, dropped
it in a jar of jasmine tea
which three hours in the freezer turned to rock.

On our first walk I plucked a fern,
arranged it in a cast full of hot wax.
Now the candle is almost burnt
away, a hard miniature pool acts
as evidence on a plate, a spell
cast and lost on a pagoda shell.

Art Work

Art Deco semicircles hung from the ears
of the Stratford-on-Avon gift shop lady
like the ones you died in when your car veered
onto the sheer part of the valley's cradle.
Had you seen the twisted wires which held you down
you would have wanted to take them home with you
to add to your rows of mesh dragons and crowns,
half-glazed pots, glass jars full of brushes and glue,
the rare cocktails of murky water and paint,
cork rescued from prevailing winds, an owl's skull,
meticulously sorted driftwood and chains:
the treasures of a still life by water's lull.

Stratford-on-Avon: where you had your ears pierced
in 1955 on a day trip from school.

Abortion

It is a blemish on paper
we don't notice, an inherited watermark
in the heart. We know she took
the stated dose, the colours of the tablets
a palette, her horsehair brushes
untouched in the drawer as a prayerbook.
We become involved with doctors
as convolvulus. Every day is
turning a page in a medical dictionary.
We should leave logarithms to themselves,
repent of the past like an undug garden.
Prescriptions? False rhetoric.
Let's talk about morphine.

The Breakdown

for David Helfgott

I emerge from the velvet drapes
like a king. The piano is ready,
black and polished as a coffin.
I want to climb into its open back
and pull the lid down, but I know
it will not swallow me whole. My torture
is to be of a different kind — note by note until
there is no more sound, only the flat tapping
of someone trying to get me out.

I sit at the keyboard
imagining the seascape I am to
sculpt from these black and white blocks.
All the violins turn to me like arrows.
The silence tightens
as if a gunman had centred his target.
I nod and begin. My fingers tantalise
the keys. A string is cut. I am free.
I give my soul to the notes. It is perfect.
I take off, feet folded in, wings whole and flowing.
Below me the tigers smile. They want
my bones, but I am going higher and higher.
I am with the notes. They will not catch me,
the tigers in their suits below.

I do not recognise the movement
of those hands. They are so taut and raw.
I'm up in the dome. Below
they are mesmerised. I hear nothing but
flat tapping on wet keys. At the crescendo I zoom
into the fingers as if they are gloves.
It is the end. I stand. There is clapping. My head
hits the lid. A light goes out. The orchestra bends
over me like a group of designated mourners.

White, white, green. The Rach III. Free,
in a white gown. Who are these, the green-masked
who tie me down, thread strings through my skin,
their instruments off key in metal bowls?
Are they playing the Rach III on me? Did I
crash into the dome on the way up
and out? Perhaps the tigers sank their teeth
in too deep. Am I to be inscribed,
petrified on a page by these
whose mouths are bound?

When the white bolts shoot through
me, I am not here
on this steel bed.
I am with the notes,
up in the dome.
I am the Rach III.

Labyrinthitis —
Ariadne's 115th Dream Revisited

Here we go again — hand me the wool.
It's north by north-west and mind
the holes on Corner Twelve. Heavy breathing
means he's five hundred yards away
and I must cut my hands searching
for crevices to conceal myself, already
three times concealed. To become interstitial
by default is a matter of genetics.
My pursuit is of a monstrance pointing
its twelve fingers from the high altar down,
not centaur-wise by clock-light round.

Deaf. No longer do I see red;
I hear it in my eyes, its decibel
a souvenir. To know whole symphonies
only as an echo in an architrave
in my head, a primary source in the fog,
is merely a tribute to sound,
like where there were once words
in the sand.

Find my way out? No way, Treeport, there is no
halberdier strong enough to cut this half-beast
trunk down. Bad circulation in here: triangular
throbbing. I hear a string drawn across a bow.
        Don't shoot
me, arrow-tongued monster, don't cut my ears
out, a Philomel, and send them recorded
delivery to Theseus, silver octaves
in daguerreotype, plain as the harbour lights
doomed in white. Doing my ward rounds
now — place your bets. Mine's extra-marine
with ice.

Stranded on Ithaca

I

The day she went over the edge
she was wearing red.
The car struck ice at eighty
and then it was down,
down to the seabed.
The third rebound rocked
contortions of fear
across the wing mirror, a forty foot drop
off a bridge, the road gaping below,
and then Ithaca.

Life, a home movie in reverse
unexpurgated in the dark
on the windscreen. The smithereens
a handful of teeth, the Jack of Hearts.
Then the muted incunabula of love
lining the mind: the first ten years
she'd played poker every night
with her three hundred suitors
over roasted pig — small solace
for being entombed with a view
from a white-washed palace.
So many men, so little wine.
Only her late-night unravellings and azure tears
labelled in phials in the boudoir
had told the tale of her ten-year traveller,
Big Jim, still haunted on Boreatic seas.

II

The door jammed. Earth
in place of sky. Straightening her tiara she
pulls the gauze veil from the glove compartment
and floats out. All around the islands
loom and pass among the icebergs.

The sea horses dip and curl. Their murky
shells resent a lost sea-kingdom
where I hear a dirge inviting me
to re-invent my coral hand. I'm in Recovery
on the back seat with Duke C
and his malignant crew — then the surge
comes down, wiring me up
to the floor. The ultrasonographer
hallucinates behind the door
disguising the signs. *Straight on!*
he shouts, *straight on!*
I try re-wind. But I can't find
the gear. Wrong side.
Now I'm in Discovery
Room. Electroconvulsive waves
hit me, shredding my tongue. Maybe
if I press pause. I'll have time
to prise the tumours out. Too late.
I can't erase the phrase. In time
with the sound of the five pines
outside the window, my bony fingers
tap the steering wheel, my shield.
No relic this, no simple twist
of the neck for effect. Only the king
out all night on deck counting his
razor blades. Cut to fade.

No trace left. Unclear
this fear that tilts my coronet
and spears my side, the fish that peer
into my eyes, and eat them. Those are pearls
that were his. Nobody knows
I am composed as a princess
on a surgeon's bed, my long wound
teeming with turquoise scales.
Bracken haemorrhages
through the rear window
as I press fast forward.
Stop. June, the hour
of the new moon, the bloom of hawthorn
beneath my feet. I clutch the seaweed
and accelerate.

III

There's no seating plan, only calligraphy
and the rest is turning as the lute
music struggles watery and out of tune
on the radio. I unpick the shroud
and now I'm out. *That's not allowed*
they said, *IT'S NOT ALLOWED.*
The scribes, they got it wrong.
They always do. My trouble, doctor, is
I'm still behind that wheel
keeling over into another field.

Not into lipreading.
It's all gunpowder and caster sugar
at midnight. Except you don't always
notice the scars. The car's
the same in my head. But I went through
the sun-roof, came back from the dead
and sang the *Salve* backwards
before they scrolled me down
and pulled the scalpel out.

Understanding the Echo

Understanding the echo is the hardest part
of being young, its faint notes
pure and reedy in an empty hall.

I'm anaesthetizing the sky
and trying to listen to the voice
of the stars and decipher the trembling
of chandeliers and the colour blue.

Last time I came alive I brushed
the seaweed from my eyes,
peeled my sticky scales
and heard the dim boom beckoning.
But the sea is its own grave.

Leaving Bird Rock

Where you plunge below crags,
heather-coated sheep devour
a mountainside falling
into the sea. Sheer cliff face
splices seaweed into unconscious-
ness until an acre becomes an inch
between finger and thumb on the rim
of the hot air balloon.

The Truth About Escalators

You can risk nothing with escalators.
They flow to the floor below,

their neat teeth pulling you down,
down. Rectagular waves

blend into an estuary of the bodiless
on rails. I feel myself hanging

among them while you go on
without me. Soon I will never see you

again: you will slip into a glass underworld
while I miss my step up here.

They are as beguiling as metronomes,
seeming to bring us closer as we move

further apart and each floor pours
us onto new levels of loss. Although

you are only one step away,
my personal space can never spill over

into yours: harmony is precisely
what keeps us apart.

There is no going back.
The escalator decides for us.

Acknowledgements

Acknowledgements are due to the editors of the following publications where some of these poems first appeared: *Poetry Wales, The Independent, Oxygen* (Seren, ed. Amy Wack & Grahame Davies, 2000), *Stranded on Ithaca* (Redbeck Press, 1998), *Traveller's Moon* (Aural Images, ed. Alan White, 1997).

Special thanks to tutors at Tŷ Newydd Writing Centre, especially Robert Minhinnick for his encouragement.